SandCastle™

Team Sports
By the Numbers

Basketball
By the Numbers

Mary Elizabeth Salzmann

Consulting Editor, Diane Craig, M.A./Reading Specialist

ABDO
Publishing Company

Published by ABDO Publishing Company, 8000 West 78th Street, Edina, Minnesota 55439.

Copyright © 2010 by Abdo Consulting Group, Inc. International copyrights reserved in all countries.

No part of this book may be reproduced in any form without written permission from the publisher. SandCastle™ is a trademark and logo of ABDO Publishing Company.

Printed in the United States.

 PRINTED ON RECYCLED PAPER

Editor: Katherine Hengel
Content Developer: Nancy Tuminelly
Cover and Interior Design and Production: Colleen Dolphin, Mighty Media
Photo Credits: iStockphoto (Rob Friedman, Lawrence Sawyer), Shutterstock

Library of Congress Cataloging-in-Publication Data

Salzmann, Mary Elizabeth, 1968-
  Basketball by the numbers / Mary Elizabeth Salzmann.
     p. cm. -- (Team sports by the numbers)
  ISBN 978-1-60453-768-0
  1. Basketball--Juvenile literature. I. Title.
  GV885.1.S25 2010
  796.323--dc22
                              2009025764

SandCastle™ Level: Transitional

SandCastle™ books are created by a team of professional educators, reading specialists, and content developers around five essential components—phonemic awareness, phonics, vocabulary, text comprehension, and fluency—to assist young readers as they develop reading skills and strategies and increase their general knowledge. All books are written, reviewed, and leveled for guided reading, early reading intervention, and Accelerated Reader® programs for use in shared, guided, and independent reading and writing activities to support a balanced approach to literacy instruction. The SandCastle™ series has four levels that correspond to early literacy development. The levels are provided to help teachers and parents select appropriate books for young readers.

Emerging Readers
(no flags)

Beginning Readers
(1 flag)

Transitional Readers
(2 flags)

Fluent Readers
(3 flags)

SandCastle™ would like to hear from you. Please send us your comments and suggestions.
sandcastle@abdopublishing.com

Contents

Introduction.. 4

The Basketball Court 5

The Game.. 6

Offense... 9

Defense 17

Basketball Facts 22

Answers to By the Numbers!........................... 23

Glossary... 24

Introduction

Numbers are used all the time in basketball.

- Free throws are worth 1 point.

- A basketball is 29.5 inches (75 cm) around.

- A player who makes 6 fouls has to sit out for the rest of the game.

- The free throw line is 15 feet (4.5 m) from the basket.

- A basketball hoop is 10 feet (3 m) high.

- An **overtime** period lasts 5 minutes.

Let's see how else numbers are used in basketball.

50 feet (15 m)

15 feet (4.5 m)

12 feet (3.6 m)

The Basketball Court

94 feet (29 m)

The Game

In basketball, there are 5 players on each team.

A basketball game lasts 60 minutes. The game is **divided** into quarters. Each quarter has 15 minutes.

After halftime, the teams **switch** baskets.

Offense

The team trying to score is the offense.

Dominic **dribbles** the basketball down the court. He will try to score a basket.

By the Numbers!

A Dominic has already scored 6 points. If he makes another basket, he will score 2 more points. How many total points will he have scored?

(answer on p. 23)

Maya wants to pass the ball to a teammate.

Caleb shoots the basketball. He wants to score points to help his team win the game.

By the Numbers!

C Caleb's team has 10 points. The other team has 8 points. How many more points does Caleb's team have?

(answer on p. 23)

14

Kim was fouled by a player on the other team. She gets to take a free throw.

By the Numbers!

(D) Kim scored 2 points for making the basket when she was fouled. If she makes the free throw, she'll get 1 more point. How many points will she have scored on the play?

(answer on p. 23)

Defense

The team trying to keep the other team from scoring is the defense.

Mary tries to steal the ball from Ella.

By the Numbers!

E Mary has stolen the ball 3 times. Other players on her team have stolen the ball 6 times. How many steals does Mary's team have?

(answer on p. 23)

Chris reaches up to block Wyatt's shot. He tries to touch only the ball so he won't foul Wyatt.

By the Numbers!

F

It takes 6 fouls to foul out. Chris has 4 fouls. He will foul out if he makes how many more fouls?

(answer on p. 23)

Cody missed his shot. Juan will try to get the **rebound**.

By the Numbers!

G

Juan has 5 rebounds. If he gets another one, how many rebounds will he have?

(answer on p. 23)

Basketball Facts

- The National Basketball Association was formed in 1949.

- In the 1960s the Boston Celtics won the NBA **Championship** 8 years in a row.

- In 1962 Wilt Chamberlain scored 100 points in one game.

- Kareem Abdul-Jabbar scored 38,387 points in his NBA **career**.

- The 3-point line was added in 1979.

- Yao Ming is 7 feet, 6 inches (2.3 m) tall.

- In 1983, the Detroit Pistons beat the Denver Nuggets 186 to 184.

- Michael Jordan and Wilt Chamberlain both averaged more than 30 points per game.

Answers to By the Numbers!

D

$$\begin{array}{r} 2 \\ +1 \\ \hline 3 \end{array}$$

Kim scored 2 points for making the basket when she was fouled. If she makes the free throw, she'll get 1 more point. How many points will she have scored on the play?

A

$$\begin{array}{r} 6 \\ +2 \\ \hline 8 \end{array}$$

Dominic has already scored 6 points. If he makes another basket, he will score 2 more points. How many total points will he have scored?

E

$$\begin{array}{r} 3 \\ +6 \\ \hline 9 \end{array}$$

Mary has stolen the ball 3 times. Other players on her team have stolen the ball 6 times. How many steals does Mary's team have?

B

$$\begin{array}{r} 4 \\ -3 \\ \hline 1 \end{array}$$

Maya has 4 teammates. Players on the other team are guarding 3 of them. How many of her teammates are open to catch Maya's pass?

F

$$\begin{array}{r} 6 \\ -4 \\ \hline 2 \end{array}$$

It takes 6 fouls to foul out. Chris has 4 fouls. He will foul out if he makes how many more fouls?

C

$$\begin{array}{r} 10 \\ -8 \\ \hline 2 \end{array}$$

Caleb's team has 10 points. The other team has 8 points. How many more points does Caleb's team have?

G

$$\begin{array}{r} 5 \\ +1 \\ \hline 6 \end{array}$$

Juan has 5 **rebounds**. If he gets another one, how many rebounds will he have?

Glossary

career – the work or jobs done over a period of time.

championship – a series of games played to decide which team is the best.

divided – separated into groups or parts.

dribble – to continually bounce a basketball with one hand.

overtime – an extra period of a sport that is played if the score is tied when the regular time is over.

rebound – the act of catching a basketball after it has bounced off the hoop or backboard.

switch – to change places or take turns.

To see a complete list of SandCastle™ books and other nonfiction titles from ABDO Publishing Company, visit www.abdopublishing.com.
8000 West 78th Street, Edina, MN 55439 • 800-800-1312 • fax 952-831-1632